Original title:
Voices Behind the Walls

Copyright © 2025 Creative Arts Management OÜ
All rights reserved.

Author: Adrian Caldwell
ISBN HARDBACK: 978-1-80587-017-3
ISBN PAPERBACK: 978-1-80587-487-4

The Chronicles of the Unheard

In corners where shadows dance and prance,
A chorus of whispers takes its chance.
They tell of socks that utterly flee,
And of cats with grand dreams of being free.

A potato once thought it could sing,
But it found the stage much less of a thing.
It rolled off the counter, gave quite a scare,
Proving it's safer, just not to dare.

Behind every cabinet, a tale awaits,
Of mismatched shoes and disappearing plates.
The radio hums a sweet little tune,
While the fridge has a joke that makes you swoon.

The laundry room giggles, it's quite the mess,
Fights over who has the fluffiest dress.
And in this odd realm, joy's easy to find,
For laughter's a language that's wholly unconfined.

The Weight of Suppressed Stories

The cat on the rooftop sings a tune,
While the dog below just howls at the moon.
Socks have their secrets, they hide in the draw,
Pants tell no tales, but they sure have their flaw.

A goldfish in bubbles thinks it's a star,
Dancing in water, it's a true, fancy car.
Llamas in pajamas whisper jokes on the hay,
I'm laughing so hard, I might float away.

Garnets of Unheard Songs

Noses in corners, they burp tiny tunes,
Frogs croak in chorus, like old-time loons.
A toaster pops bread, just like it's a show,
And crumbling cookies want everyone to know.

Balloons filled with giggles are floating so high,
While the fridge hums a melody, oh my!
Couches are plush, yet they snicker in glee,
When people sit down for a snack with more spree.

The Abode of Gentle Whispers

In a corner, the ceiling fan starts to spin,
It chats with the light bulb about who can win.
A turtle in slippers narrates by the door,
While the broom in the closet dreams of the floor.

Chairs play poker and shuffle their legs,
While crumbs on the table make bets with the eggs.
Each tick of the clock is a chuckle or sigh,
As shadows debate if they should say bye.

Soliloquies within Shadows

A shadow on the wall does pretzel routines,
While candy wrappers whisper of sweet little dreams.
The chairs giggle softly at gossip of old,
As rugs plot a dance to the stories they're told.

A paperclip's wink has a mischievous tone,
While a lamp weighs in like it's made of fine stone.
Footprints in dust have a mystery deep,
In this lonesome abode where secrets still creep.

When Silence Starts to Speak

In the corner, a sock just grins,
Whispers of lost shoes and dusty bins.
The fridge hums a tune so sweet,
It dances while we munch on meat.

A tap on the sink starts to giggle,
As pots and pans playing a riddle.
The couch creaks with secrets to tell,
While catnip dreams cast their spell.

The Unraveling of Echoed Tales

A chair wobbles, 'Hey, hold my drink!'
The ghost of snacks past starts to wink.
As the dust motes plot their next joke,
With laughter that's barely bespoke.

The mirror chuckles, showing a grin,
Reflecting the chaos, where to begin?
Tales of socks lost in the fight,
Spinning their yarns every night.

Secret Hymns of the Abandoned

Old toys chatter in the dim light,
Singing their songs of delight.
Puzzles whisper, 'We still connect,'
While empty bottle dreams can reflect.

A ladder leans, rusted and proud,
Reciting its childhood dreams aloud.
Frameless photos hop with glee,
Telling wild stories, just wait and see.

Soft Footfalls of the Unvoiced

A mouse clicks, 'Did someone just sneeze?'
Lurking in corners, they aim to please.
The clock ticks, 'Time for a joke,'
As shadows giggle, pretending to cloak.

A blanket whispers, 'Come take a seat,'
While every creak keeps a steady beat.
And when night falls, they come alive,
With every chuckle, they start to thrive.

Canvases of Quietude

In the corners where shadows creep,
Whispers of laughter, secrets to keep.
A cat in a hat sings a tune,
While the goldfish dances to the moon.

Pictures hang with a magical flair,
While dust bunnies start their ballet in air.
Chairs with stories, they wiggle and sway,
As if plotting mischief for the day.

Fragments of Solitary Songs

Upstairs, the sock monkey tells a tale,
Of a brave toaster who set sail.
Each pop and each crunch is a cheer,
As crumbs applaud with a friendly sneer.

Behind the door, a forgotten broom,
Practices tango in the dim light's gloom.
With every twist and every spin,
Chortles erupt from within.

The Language of Forgotten Corners

In nooks where dust gathers and sleeps,
The old clock laughs while the shadow peeps.
A teacup grins, snug in its place,
As spoons gossip with a clinking grace.

Beneath the sink lives a wise old sponge,
Who tells tales of parties, wild and grunge.
Each puddle echoes a splashing jest,
As forks fandango, feeling blessed.

Resonance of the Invisible

Echoes ricochet like light on a spree,
As a rogue pencil doodles the sea.
The rug hums jokes about the shoes,
While the wallpaper sings boisterous blues.

Beneath the bed, where dreams have a ball,
A mismatched sock hosts a grand hall.
With chuckles and hiccups, they take flight,
As the night slips into laughter and light.

Murmured Promises

In corners where shadows play,
Whispers dance and sway.
A cat in a hat, oh so spry,
Claims the couch as his favorite sky.

Old shoes with a squeak, they pact,
Conspiring to catch the act.
The baker's dough takes a leap,
While eating dreams, they giggle deep.

Lost socks hold secret schemes,
Chasing the fridge for midnight creams.
A tapestry of unseen delights,
Hums softly in the endless nights.

Behind the curtains, mischief brews,
With each tumble of secret news.
Laughter echoes in every space,
At the antics we can't replace.

An Atlas of Hidden Stories

Underneath the floorboards creak,
A tambourine plays hide and seek.
Stray pizza crusts plot their next trip,
While goldfish gather for a blip.

Maps drawn on the foggy glass,
Show pathways where time does pass.
A squirrel dreams of world tours,
While the old clock tells tales of roars.

A left sock writes a memoir grand,
About a dreamy breakfast land.
With cereal pouring all around,
In capes made of wrappers, they abound.

Faint giggles escape the room,
As toys prepare for their bloom.
An atlas of stories grows each night,
In the quiet glow of twilight.

Tales Told in the Dark

In the depths of a cloaked night,
Crickets sing with all their might.
A mouse spins yarns with flair,
While spoons frolic in midair.

Whispers clap like thunder bright,
As darkness dons its cozy light.
The moon laughs at the hoots nearby,
As owls flaunt their tired eye.

A pizza slice starts to strut,
Chasing breadcrumbs through the rut.
Old books shake off layers of dust,
Spinning tales of love and trust.

Beneath the bed, a monster waits,
For mischief the hour creates.
In this dimly lit spree,
Stories flutter wild and free.

Shades of Silent Longing

In the pantry, ghosts do waltz,
With flavors of forgotten faults.
Sugar spirits take their chance,
Turning beans into a dance.

Tales float through the air so light,
As shadows jive with pure delight.
The fridge hums a lullaby sweet,
While leftovers rise to their feet.

Lost spoons dream of silver bling,
While forks plot a golden fling.
Behind the walls, the giggles grow,
In the silence, warmth will flow.

Whimsy tugs at every heart,
As the night begins its art.
Within the calm of these hidden shows,
Longing fills the air with prose.

Murmurs in the Darkness

In shadows where giggles reside,
They whisper secrets with pride.
A sock puppet talks of a feud,
While a toaster hums, feeling rude.

The fridge claims low-fat cheese is bold,
While the kettle spills tales of old.
A broom sweeps while humming a tune,
As a lamp quips, 'I light up the room!'

Silent Chants of the Past

A chair creaks with gossip so sly,
As the clock ticks, it rolls its eye.
Walls chuckle at dust bunnies' plight,
While the carpet sighs, 'Not tonight!'

The paintings wink with frames so elaborate,
Mona Lisa giggles; she's never late.
Porcelain cats whisper love stories,
As the walls echo, lost glories.

Beneath the Surface

Under the floorboards, cats hatch a scheme,
Plotting around a sunbeam's gleam.
The vacuum rolls in, causing a ruckus,
While a mop grumbles, 'Now, that's just nuts!'

Beneath the surface, they jive and prance,
With a broomstick leading a crazy dance.
Old shoes reminisce of the days they trod,
While a doormat sighs, 'I've seen quite a lot!'

They Speak

The old couch grumbles 'I need a break!'
'What's a chair without me?' it shakes.
As the curtains exchange funny looks,
With stories hidden in dusty books.

The fridge is a gossip, oh what a beast,
Reportedly loving late-night feast.
The blender buzzes with untold delight,
While the microwave chimes, 'Just heat it right!'

Stories Entombed in Silence

In the attic, where silence blooms,
A box whispers tales of dusty rooms.
The bicycle sulks, rusted and sad,
While a rocking horse is grinning glad.

The grandfather clock chimes jokester wise,
Counting the minutes with glittering eyes.
Old toys conspire, plotting their fun,
As the daylight fades, their stories begun.

Murals of the Unspoken

In the corner, a cat whispers,
As it plots with the shadows, oh what a mess!
The walls giggle with old tales,
While the door sings tuneless but happy tales.

Chairs gossip about how they're sat on,
While the fridge hums its cool, frosty song,
A sock on the floor holds court in delight,
It claims it's the king of the laundry plight.

Windows chuckle at the clouds' silly shapes,
While potted plants swap dirt and some grapes,
The clock ticks in rhythm, a dance in place,
It's late for a meeting but stuck in this space.

Underneath the stairs, a broom tells a joke,
In dusty corners, the laughter provokes,
With every creak, the floorboards respond,
To the unseen crowd that's hidden beyond.

Dichotomies of Silence

Silence speaks loud in a muffled way,
Like a grumpy snail on a slow, long day,
Where the wallpaper beams with playful hues,
And candy wrappers share their news.

A toaster pops out tales of burnt bread,
With crumbs that sing songs of days long fled,
While the curtains sway in a breeze quite bold,
Whispering secrets that never grow old.

In the attic, a ghost with a perky hat,
Stares in disbelief at a sleeping cat,
Both bewildered by the haste of life,
Where dust bunnies gather, avoiding the strife.

The couch sighs deeply, tired of the scene,
It dreams of adventures, oh, to be seen,
Through giggles of silence, we laugh with glee,
Who knew the quiet could be so carefree?

Sounds of the Dimly Lit

A lamp flickers a joke, just to please,
While shadows dance with the utmost ease,
Muffled whispers float on through the night,
Wrapped up in blankets, they giggle in fright.

The refrigerator's hum keeps the rhythm alive,
A beat to which all the dust bunnies thrive,
Cobwebs giggle as they sway and spin,
In the glow of dusk, the fun will begin.

Socks hiding 'neath beds share secrets galore,
Afraid of the washing machine evermore,
A toothpaste tube sighs, it's always last,
Yet still finds a way to have a laugh blast.

In corners where darkness and fun collide,
Furry critters chime in, nowhere to hide,
As laughter echoes through the dimly lit,
In shadows and light, they never quit.

Reflections in the Quiet

Mirrors grin back with a cheeky glance,
Each crack a story of life's strange dance,
Echoes of giggles paint the air bright,
In hues of mischief, they take their flight.

Potted plants eavesdrop on tales of the stove,
Where dinner attempts find a humorous grove,
Spices in jars whisper laughter so bold,
Sharing a jest that's covered in gold.

The clock on the wall ticks a sly little tune,
Counting the moments till they burst into June,
As shadows debate who'll win the night's race,
In this quiet abode, there's a playful embrace.

With a swish of the broom, the dust spins in glee,
Joining the laughter, so wild and so free,
In reflections of silence, the fun comes alive,
In this world of the quiet, where chuckles thrive.

Lament of the Forgotten

In the attic, a sock took flight,
Singing tales of laundry night.
The cat joined in, with a purr so sly,
Even the dust bunnies waved goodbye.

A spoon chimed in with a silver tune,
While the lamp hummed bright like a cheeky moon.
Old books whispered secrets from their shelf,
As I chuckled alone, just me and myself.

The fridge played notes of yogurt's despair,
While the leftovers groaned, warning beware!
A dance party erupted, no one in sight,
With forgotten friends of the food pyramid height.

Behind the door, a vacuum sneezed,
Dust motes spun in the air, quite pleased.
Who knew the walls had such a flair?
In the forgotten nooks, life was rare.

Chants of the Silent

At night, the clock softly ticks,
Counting giggles, chalking tricks.
In the dark, a pencil scribbles a plot,
While the old chair creaks, "Give it a shot!"

Empty mugs began to confer,
"Who's due a refill?" asked the stirrer.
The curtains swayed, a playful breeze,
Acting like dancers with utmost ease.

Floorboards whispered of tales untold,
Of sock puppets and action figures bold.
They plotted escape with a flimsy string,
While I just sat, enjoying the fling.

An old broom chuckled, dusted away,
"Mop's on vacation, let's dance, hooray!"
Each corner held its secret bliss,
But they all knew they'd be missed.

The Language of Seclusion

Beneath the sink lived a rubber duck,
Who dreamed of swimming, good luck!
With a quack of laughter, it spread delight,
Spilling soap bubbles under a midnight light.

A toaster popped, with a grin so wide,
Cheering for crumbs that had nowhere to hide.
The kettle echoed a bubbling cheer,
While the microwave giggled, "Whatcha got in here?"

The cupboard held a secret stash,
Of spices with flair, a zesty clash.
They squabbled over flavors, they jived,
In a culinary rave, they thrived.

A lonely chair squeaked a tune,
Waiting for friends to join the afternoon.
But in the silence, their laughter soared,
In a room full of chatter, they were adored.

Songs of the Invisible

An old shoe grinned, its laces tied,
"Mismatched is best," it joked with pride.
The carpet chuckled, hiding crumbs,
While a rogue flea danced, playing drums.

The light switch flip-flopped with glee,
Sparking joy for all to see.
Wallflowers echoed, "Let's throw a ball!"
And the floor, well, just took the fall.

Back in the shadows, the paint peeled grace,
Bravely revealing its colorful face.
The doorbell giggled, a cheeky chime,
Saying, "I'm here, give me a time!"

In every nook, a surprise to find,
The walls kept secrets, playful and kind.
With laughter echoing, no need to fuss,
In the quiet corners, a living must.

Tales Caught in the Air

Balloons whisper secrets, floating so high,
A cat in a hat dreams of tasting the sky.
The neighbor's old parrot sings tunes from the past,
While squirrels debate how long winter will last.

Gossipy shadows play tag on the floor,
A chair gives a creak, 'Who let in the bore?'
Mice scribble stories, in the pantry they dwell,
While thunder applauds their mischievous spell.

Raccoons in tuxedos toss crumbs of delight,
As owls wear monocles, reading all night.
Each gust of the wind, a tale on the breeze,
Curious whispers float through the trees.

So listen closely, lean in with a grin,
For stories abound even when days grow thin.
Where laughter is born from the quirkiest dealings,
Catch a giggle that's lost in the feel of good feelings.

The Scent of Forgotten Memories

The closet emits a whiff of old cheese,
As socks have debates with the jackets with ease.
Old photographs giggle, they speak of the past,
While moths in top hats dance slow, but not fast.

Dust bunnies gather for tea on the floor,
Each with a tale of what once was before.
The mirror reflects a face wearing a grin,
As echoes of laughter drift softly within.

A sock puppet rises, declares it's a king,
Proclaims all lost memories have something to bring.
With scents of old spices, the walls join the fun,
Reminiscing of days when they basked in the sun.

So come take a whiff, let your worries all fly,
Among quirky old relics that never ask why.
In this kingdom of laughter, of scents and delight,
Forgotten memories join in, both day and night.

Reveries in the Gloom

In the corner, a chair plots a scheme,
While shadows rehearse for their nightly dream.
A blanket whispers jokes, it's cozy and warm,
Laughing at stories that weather each storm.

The clock on the wall counts down to its show,
While curtains discuss how their colors should flow.
With whispers of mischief, the darkness takes flight,
As glow-in-the-dark stars giggle with delight.

Posters from the past giggle and cheer,
Reminding us gently there's nothing to fear.
A dinosaur rummages through a lost book,
While the light bulb is dying, but won't let it cook.

So dance in the dim, embrace all that's near,
With laughter dripping sweet, let go of all fear.
For even in gloom, joy can spark and ignite,
In the curious corners where shadows delight.

Lullabies of the Isolated

Under the bed, a rumble of cheer,
As dust motes waltz lightly, drawing us near.
A teddybear croons to the dolls in a line,
Sweet melodies drifting through space and through time.

The windowpanes chatter, exchanging their hues,
While curtains spread gossip, sharing the news.
The floorboards join in with a creaky old tune,
As crickets hold concerts beneath a warm moon.

An echoing giggle floats up from the stairs,
While imaginary friends play games without cares.
An orchestra of silence that tickles and woos,
In the kingdom of laughter where everyone snooze.

So nestle your head, let worries take flight,
With lullabies sung by the stars every night.
For nestled in shadows, fun waits to be found,
In the sweetest of dreams where joy knows no bounds.

Shadows of Untold Tales

In the attic, dust bunnies laugh,
A ghost in a hat trying to do maths.
Old paintings wink, revealing the truth,
While chairs gossip about their lost youth.

A cat with a monocle sips on some tea,
With secrets of muffins that once flew free.
Eerie giggles echo, a stand-up routine,
As shadows play charades, a hilarious scene.

Mops dance in circles, and brooms waltz by,
As cobwebs provide a soft, silky tie.
The clock chimes a joke with a tick and a tock,
While old socks plot a great fashion shock.

In corners reside the lost marbles of fate,
That giggle at stories left far too late.
The walls have a rhythm, a comedic sway,
As shadows of laughter abound every day.

Notes from the Other Side

On the other side of the creaky old door,
A toaster tells tales of bread that once swore.
Jars in the cupboard giggle at snails,
While spoons share their dreams of wild, wavy trails.

The vacuum whispers secrets of crumbs,
Of daring expeditions, and lost gum chews.
In the fridge, a pickle starts a raucous fight,
With mustard defending its condimental right.

Chairs conspire to change their old seat,
While wigs on the shelf plan a wild street beat.
A teapot recounts all its steeping escapes,
And a cheese grater dreams of stylish capes.

Pans rattle together with humorous glee,
As they plot the next feast of pure jubilee.
With laughter echoing across the divide,
These whimsical notes from where laughter resides.

Ripples of Resilience

In the pond of the backyard, frogs wear their crowns,
Hopping in sync to the silliest sounds.
Tadpoles are plotting to start a new craze,
While lilies are whispering secrets and ways.

The breeze tells a story, a giggly swoosh,
As daisies sway, making humor a push.
The fish in a frenzy perform little flips,
While snails hold a rally, exchanging fun quips.

Bubbles break free, like laughter in air,
As ripples emerge, now they're here, now they're there.
They travel through puddles, creating a whirl,
Explaining the giggles that make colors swirl.

As the sun beams down with a whimsical wink,
The garden is buzzing, encouraging to think.
It's all in the laughter, in the moments so bright,
Where resilience thrives in the joy of the light.

Whispers from the Enclosed

Inside the cupboard, a biscuit's delight,
Chortles with chocolate in the fading light.
The jars of jam gossip, spreading tales thick,
While crumbs on the floor plan a stage for a flick.

Behind the pantry, a pickle's bold stand,
As pasta and sauce form an unlikely band.
Cereal boxes blare news in a crunch,
While fruits in a bowl share a raucous brunch.

The fridge hums a tune, a rhythmic play,
While eggs practice drama, come what may.
Lettuce holds court with a crisp, leafy grin,
As veggies unite for a veggie-filled spin.

In this world of the closed, hilarity reigns,
With laughter so loud, it spills out of chains.
So, open the doors, let the stories unfold,
As whispers of joy in the mundane are told.

Faint Calls from the Cellar

In the cellar, whispers play,
Mice gossip about the day.
Unearthed socks and dusty shoes,
Echoed laughter brings the blues.

Bubbles popping in the brew,
Cobwebs dance like they're brand new.
A rogue potato slips and slides,
While ghosts of dinner parties bide.

Spiders tell of ancient trends,
While lost hope in the dark descends.
Old wine bottles start to hum,
Who knew silence could be fun?

So if you hear a cheeky jest,
Or a gurgle, don't be stressed.
The cellar's alive, it paints a scene,
Of echoes, snacks, and something green.

The Sound of Solitude

Alone in a room, too quiet to bear,
The clock ticks loudly—oh, what a scare!
A chair creaks loud, like a mean old troll,
Reminding me to eat, or lose control.

Dust bunnies gather, in a conga line,
Debating the merits of meal times divine.
Socks play tag behind the door's moan,
Making the walls feel less alone.

The fridge hums softly, singing its tune,
"Leftover pizza, your heart is immune!"
A laugh erupts from the pot on the stove,
As noodles wiggle—they crave to rove.

In quietness, joy can be found,
Even when it's spinning all around.
So let the echoes dance and sway,
Finding humor in disarray.

Caged Melodies of Memory

In corners dark and shadows long,
A broom sings out a swaying song.
Old echoes from a time gone by,
Tickle through the dust, and fly.

Photographs with silly grins,
Laughing loudly through the sins.
The old TV wheezes a vintage tune,
As chairs start boogieing to swoon.

Memories trapped in corners tight,
Dance around in the pale moonlight.
Forgotten toys emerge to cry,
"To play with us is to testify!"

Still in the cage of time and dust,
Laughter breaks forth—a joyful thrust.
Even in stillness, we can play,
Finding fun in yesterday.

Portals of the Overlooked

Behind the door, a treasure pings,
Socks and lost change wear ring-a-dings.
A cat's eye peeks from a cupboard high,
Don't let it fool you, it's just a spy!

The closet cackles, clothing it mocks,
The winter coats don't match their socks.
A shoe attempts to dance on its own,
Stomping loudly on the wayward bone.

Curtains flutter in an unseen breeze,
Whispering jokes that aim to please.
The stale perfume, a dating flop,
Comes strutting forth, "Here I am, stop!"

In hidden corners, we find delight,
Where whispers laugh and shadows bite.
Open the doors, let the fun ignite,
In overlooked places, there's pure light.

Remnants of Testimonies

Whispers dance like dust in air,
Promises made in a secret lair.
Echoes of laughter, tales untold,
Rumors rise like bread, fresh and bold.

Chairs creak under heavy sighs,
A cat knocks over a stack of pies.
Jokes exchanged with a knowing wink,
Time to toast with a silly clink!

Old photos smirk from the wall,
As shadows stretch and start to sprawl.
Grandpa's mustache winks with glee,
While Auntie spins tales sipping sweet tea.

In the corners, secrets peek,
Silly dances, legacies speak.
Laughter bursts like popcorn rain,
In this haven, joy remains!

The Poetry Within the Grains

In the attic, dust bunnies play,
Whispering secrets, day after day.
Grains of laughter float on the breeze,
Tickling memories, like leaves from trees.

Nuts and bolts sing a rusty tune,
While mice in the corner plot by the moon.
A cookie jar grins, almost alive,
Sharing sweet stories, keeping alive.

Straw hats sprawled, on the shelf called fate,
Chatting 'bout dreams that couldn't wait.
"Who knew a pantry could hold such lore?"
As forks and spatulas humor galore!

Among the cobwebs, laughter's entwined,
Tickles of mischief, nearly unconfined.
In every grain, a giggle, a cheer,
Old furniture whispers, "Stay cozy, my dear."

Muted Cries of the Heart

Beneath the surface, a giggle brews,
A heart that whispers, in playful hues.
Silent sighs wearing joyful masks,
As teacups gossip and sunshine basks.

Puppy eyes peek from behind the chair,
Chasing shadows without a care.
Tick-tock clocks tickle time with wit,
In muted laughter, they softly sit.

Every silence holds a chuckle bright,
The moon cracks jokes; it's quite the sight!
Waves of whimsy drown out the fear,
In hidden corners, laughter draws near.

Secrets wrap in a blanket of mirth,
Dreams dance wildly, giving birth.
To tales that twirl and swirl in the night,
Silent cries soar, taking flight!

Eyes in the Dark

In shadows deep, tickles abound,
Eyes peer out without making a sound.
A lamp stumbles, and giggles unwind,
Mysteries laugh, all beautifully blind.

Whiskers twitch with a curious pout,
As midnight snacks venture out and about.
Curfew? Nah, let the fun commence,
As sleepyheads dance in their defense.

Mirrors chuckle, reflecting the jest,
While the bed creaks, taking its rest.
Whispers of mischief float through the gloom,
While starlight tumbles into the room.

And when dawn settles with a yawn,
The echoes of laughter gently fawn.
Eyes in the dark know all the tricks,
As day awakens, the laughter still kicks!

Reverberations of the Hidden

Whispers of the fridge at night,
They giggle as they chill the light.
The toaster's secrets, they all toast,
I swear they make the best of ghosts.

Underneath the stairway's chat,
The vacuum laughs at this and that.
Dust bunnies chuckle with delight,
A comedic scene in morning light.

The washing machine hums a tune,
It croons a ballad to the moon.
Socks conspire in a quiet waltz,
Joking 'bout the mess, no faults.

Stuffy rooms with laughter gleam,
As cupboards play a silly theme.
What's that? Oh just a squeaky chair,
No haunting here, just fluff and air.

Lament of the Unseen

A creaky floorboard sighs and moans,
It tells the tale of ancient bones.
But really, it's just seeking fame,
Every creak a part of its game.

The spider spins with elegance,
In webs of mischief, full of chance.
It giggles as it catches flies,
Crafting tales beneath the skies.

The attic whispers jokes so dry,
With dusty books that seem to cry.
They chuckle at their worn-out text,
A funny plight, they feel perplexed.

In shadows that move from room to room,
Are just the cats plotting their doom.
Silly antics they perform,
While humans sleep, they're far from warm.

Ghosts of Unheard Words

A dusty shelf holds stories rare,
While ghostly friends just sit and stare.
They chat about how steep the climb,
Each laugh a hiccup out of time.

A windowpane shakes with delight,
As laughter dances into the night.
The curtains flutter, a playful wink,
Filling the room with thoughts to think.

Chairs rock gently, join the jest,
As pillows plan their fun-filled quest.
Each echo sounds both near and far,
It's ghostly humor's shining star.

In corners dark, they share a snack,
A feast of giggles, there's no lack.
The clock ticks on, but time stands still,
As unseen pals give us a thrill.

Echo Chamber of Dreams

Within the walls, a raucous cheer,
Bouncing off corners, crystal clear.
The furniture joins in the fun,
A playful dance has just begun.

The mirror winks with gleeful glee,
As shadows shape a jamboree.
Each wall suggests a secret trick,
A silent game of charades, quick!

Pots and pans in harmony sing,
Trading tales of the evening fling.
With every clang, a punchline's born,
Within this circle, laughter's worn.

A gentle breeze sweeps through the air,
It carries laughter from somewhere.
The night is filled with whispered dreams,
As walls relay their playful schemes.

Songs of the Dispossessed

In the attic, a cat sings loud,
Scratching cushions, oh so proud.
The laughter echoes off the shelves,
As I dance alone, just myself.

The fridge hums a jazzy tune,
While the dust bunnies start to croon.
I swear the slippers have a beat,
As they tap around my bare feet.

The curtains whisper silly rhymes,
About lost socks and forgotten times.
The toaster pops like fireworks bright,
In this silly, cozy night.

With every creak and every sigh,
I hear the walls chuckle and cry.
So I sing back in playful jest,
In this home, I feel so blessed.

The Cadence of Discretion

In the bathroom, the soap does glide,
A slippery secret, my personal slide.
The mirror grins with toothpaste glee,
It's my best friend; don't you see?

The shower sings a high-pitched song,
While I bob my head all day long.
The shampoo bottles dance around,
In this quirky world I've found.

The toilet's flush is quite a cheer,
A splash of laughter, never fear!
As I tiptoe on the bath mat's grin,
Each corner hides a mischievous spin.

In this room of stealthy fun,
Each scrub, each rinse, a little run.
Though sound may echo and swirl about,
I keep my secrets safe, no doubt.

Heartbeats Beneath Layers

Under the blankets, a party brews,
With socks that giggle and laughter fumes.
The pillows puff a cheeky rhyme,
As they whisper jokes in the night time.

The closet holds a shoe ballet,
As flip-flops and boots start to sway.
The dust mites throw a tiny ball,
While I listen to their tiny call.

My teddy bears begin to talk,
Sharing tales as they softly walk.
Under layers, the warmth ignites,
Creating memories of silly delights.

In this haven of snug repose,
Where hidden jokes and giggles grow.
I'll keep their secrets, warm and bright,
As heartbeats dance into the night.

Revelations in the Void

In the pantry, the biscuits plot,
Waving their crumbs with a clever knot.
The jars giggle with each twist and turn,
As I discover each flavor's yearn.

The kettle whistling a quiet tease,
As I open cupboards with surprising ease.
Each box stirs laughter, a tale to be told,
Of cupcakes gone wild and toast that's bold.

The fridge hums secrets, oh so bright,
With leftover stew and a joy for the night.
As snacks unite for a midnight feast,
Their silly antics never cease.

In this void of culinary art,
I feel the mischief tug at my heart.
With each crunch, each sip, and each treat,
I dive headfirst into absurdity sweet.

the Hushed Testament of Time.

In corners where secrets tick,
Old clocks giggle, and time goes quick.
Footsteps chase the dust around,
While shadows dance without a sound.

Laughter spills from cracked-up bricks,
As cat and mouse play silly tricks.
The walls are full of tales to tell,
With echoes that laugh and wink so well.

Jokes from the past creep through the sighs,
A ticklish breeze, oh how it flies!
Time wears a coat of chuckles and grins,
As the memories wave from their whimsical pins.

So gather round, your ears will perk,
For hidden laughs in this delightful work.
Each timeworn nook holds gags divine,
In the hush, where humor dares to shine.

Whispers in the Shadows

In the hush of night, they spill the tea,
Shadows join in a ghostly spree.
Whispers wiggle and giggle near,
Locked in chuckles, never fear.

Beneath the stairs, a snicker hides,
While mischief prances with playful strides.
A boisterous echo, a playful shout,
As the walls conspire with giggles about.

Loud shadows grinning behind the door,
With antics brewing, who'd want more?
The frail and funny run in stares,
They'll take you hostage with whimsical glares.

So lean in close and hear them weave,
Tales of giggles that never leave.
In the twilight's hugs, they prance and sway,
In the secret night, laughter has its way.

Echoes of Hidden Realms

Down the hall, a soft cackle spins,
Behind the plaster, where giggling begins.
Echoes chase the silence away,
Tickling thoughts that love to play.

In creaky floors, the humor creaks,
As ghosts exchange their silly tweaks.
A riddle wears a comical hat,
Beneath the warmth of a faded mat.

In shadowy corners, chuckles collide,
Frolicking echoes that gently glide.
Each whimpering wall, a jokester's stage,
With a script penned by a mischievous page.

The air is thick with laughter's embrace,
A treasure hunt in this playful space.
Come join the dance of clumsy cheer,
Within these echoes, fun is near.

Murmurs of the Unseen

Soft murmurs curl like fog at dusk,
Teasing faces hid with a husk.
Chubby whispers in playful rounds,
Where laughter lives upon the grounds.

A secret giggle dances free,
As jesters leap from tree to tree.
Find the sneaky snorts and squeals,
In silent rooms, where joy reveals.

These unseen murmurs tease and sing,
With a flick of a tail, they make hearts spring.
The corners smirk, with stories untold,
In this merry chase, let magic unfold.

So heed the bliss that swirls around,
In every nook where joy is found.
With silly grins and cheerful play,
The unseen mirth is here to stay.

Notes from the Inaudible

In the hush of the empty hall,
Laughter echoes, we hear a call.
Socks in the dryer, a dance they do,
No one sees their jig, but we know it's true.

The cat lounges, plotting a heist,
Dreams of stealing a fish, oh so nice.
A pot of beans simmers with glee,
Chasing the spoon, wild and free.

A tickle of dust on windowsills,
Whispers of crumbs that give us thrills.
The couch creaks—what stories it knows,
Of family gatherings and silly shows.

Chairs that groan share secret delight,
As the clock ticks softly through the night.
The fridge hums wisdom of leftovers lost,
In this quiet chaos, we pay no cost.

Thoughts Encased in the Stone

Rocks in the garden, they quietly plot,
Memory keepers of battles fought.
Each pebble a story, start to end,
Who knew boulders could be such good friends?

The old fence creaks with tales of the past,
Its boards are worn, but the humor's steadfast.
Standing guard, it's a joker at heart,
With wise cracks that never fall apart.

A squirrel chats with a rusted gate,
Trading secrets about the fate
Of the lost sandwich on the picnic table,
A quest for crumbs, if they are able.

The pavement giggles beneath our feet,
With rippling shadows, it feels so sweet.
Each crack is a wink in the midday sun,
If stones could talk, oh what fun!

Beyond Thresholds of Muteness

Behind the door, there's a party of mice,
Who nibble on cheese as if it's so nice.
They gossip and chatter in whispers and squeaks,
A kingdom of critters for days and for weeks.

The walls may seem stoic, but don't be fooled,
In the quiet, the laughter is often ruled.
A roll of the dice, a game of charades,
Adventurous spirits in playful cascades.

The lightbulb flickers like a disco beat,
As shadows sway and shuffle their feet.
They shimmy and shake past the hidden veneer,
Unseen delights linger ever so near.

Paint peels back, revealing a smile,
Alligators dance if you stay for a while.
In silence, we find a rhythm that sings,
And in this hush, let the merriment spring!

The Unwritten Chronicles

A diary of walls, tales of the board,
Of things left unsaid and laughter stored.
Each corner holds secrets, a giggle or two,
While the curtains sway like they've got a skew.

The attic whispers of baseballs and dreams,
Chess pieces plotting around moonlit beams.
Sock puppets converse on the shelf with delight,
While the old rocking chair joins in the night.

The floorboards creak like an old-time show,
Sharing old pranks only they know.
With a wink at the fridge, the toaster gives cheer,
For the toast that once went on an adventure, dear.

In a world of nooks, let laughter take flight,
With all the cheer hidden, just out of sight.
For every chuckle and grin we miss,
The chronicles play on, in fanciful bliss.

Melodies from the Depths

In a cellar, old shoes squeak,
Lizards dance, so to speak.
A pie tin sings out of tune,
While the cat hums to the moon.

Dusty boxes start to sway,
As socks debate a sock-less day.
Echoes of jugs spill a joke,
The old broom starts to croak.

Silly secrets in the cracks,
A whoopee cushion making tracks.
The cobwebs twist into clowns,
As laughter spills in hidden towns.

Between the bricks a wink goes by,
With each tickle, a chuckle flies.
Tales of fun from dusty halls,
Where silliness forever calls.

Echoes of Resilience

Behind these bricks, a dance begins,
A chorus of laughter as the fun spins.
The dishes clatter with glee and cheer,
While old chairs gossip, 'Did you hear?'

A dog starts barking at the air,
As cats join in, without a care.
The fridge hums tunes of ancient cheer,
Its shelves full of snacks, never fear.

Loud stories shared with a cheesy grin,
A sock puppet war, it's all in good skin.
Each creak of the floor joins the song,
Where silliness and joy belong.

With every rattle, a new line drawn,
In the symphony that lasts till dawn.
Behind the scenes, a ruckus swells,
As laughter and joy weave through the shells.

Notes in the Faint Breeze

A breeze flings whispers past the door,
Tickling and teasing, wanting more.
The curtains flutter in a cheeky way,
As dust motes join the grand ballet.

A squirrel gabs with a nearby crow,
Sharing secrets, not meant to show.
The old porch creaks a giggling tune,
Making up jokes with the lazy moon.

Tickle the flowers, hear them giggle,
Each petal dances with a little wiggle.
A bee buzzes a silly refrain,
While ants march in, proud of their chain.

In corners, shadows clap their hands,
Creating a show where laughter stands.
Nature's orchestra plays a bright call,
In the mingling air, to giggle, we all fall.

Chronicles of the Loudly Silent

In a nook, an echo starts to chuckle,
As mice wear hats and begin to shuffle.
Books on shelves whisper wild plots,
Where beans and peas share their sunny lots.

Beneath the stairs, a party begins,
With teddy bears claiming their wins.
Each tick of the clock plays a prank,
As the dust bunnies share a laugh at the bank.

Hidden behind doors, the fridge still hums,
While the mop drags jokes on the dusty drums.
The laughter bounces from wall to wall,
As the quiet walls host a raucous ball.

In corners where shadows softly creep,
A buzz of antics spins between sleep.
The fun within the silence grows,
In echoes of laughter, anything goes.

The Subtle Art of Reflection

In halls where echoes make their bets,
The shadows share their deepest frets.
A mirror laughs, a joke unfurls,
While dust bunnies dance in swirling whirls.

The wallpaper whispers secrets old,
Of socks lost in the couch's hold.
A cat meows like a wannabe sage,
As we query life from this funny cage.

Under the bed, what thoughts reside?
A treasure trove of dreams long denied.
A goldfish mocks from his watery throne,
While pondering why he's oft left alone.

So raise a toast to the unseen jest,
To laughter found in the hour's rest.
For every sigh that echoes through,
There's a giggle waiting, just for you!

Names Carried by the Wind

The breeze carries names like flying kites,
Some from the past, oh what funny sights!
Old Mr. Grumble with a shoe on his head,
Wonders if squirrels can count, or just spread.

A whiff of lavender scents the air,
Reviving tales of laughter we share.
With each gust that tickles our skin,
We're reminded how silly life can spin.

The clouds are our audience, giggling away,
As we trip over words we forgot to say.
The wind's our accomplice in this grand game,
Turning whispers of mischief into wild fame.

So listen closely to breezes that tease,
For they weave the tales of our lost memories.
In every chuckle the zephyrs send,
There's a reminder to laugh, to pretend!

Breaths from the Concealed

Behind closed doors, the silliness runs,
With laughter seeping through muted puns.
A sock puppet shows off his best dance moves,
While a cactus awkwardly tries to groove.

The cupboard hums with snickers disguised,
As jars of jam conspire and sized.
Each whisk of cream in the fridge twirls around,
Creating a symphony, profound but sound.

Beneath every bed, where secrets conflate,
Dust bunnies host bizarre dinner plates.
They nibble on crumbs, while plotting their scheme,
To win the award for the best funny dream.

So hold your breath and listen close,
To the chortles of those who dwell in the ghost.
For the best laughs rise up like fluffy pies,
From corners concealed, where joy never dies!

Unveiling the Hesitant

In the closet, a shy monster hides,
With unmatched socks and mismatched rides.
When doors creak open, he trembles in fright,
At the thought of being seen in the light.

His hair's a mess, like a haywire broom,
And he secretly dreams of crafting a tune.
While we tiptoe past, he clears his throat,
Then sings like a cat—so high, it could float.

Stumbling and mumbling, he gives a cheer,
For the sock that went rogue, his old dear friend here.
Together they joke 'bout the outfits they lost,
And ponder if fears are worth all the cost.

So let's pull the curtain on this funny show,
Embrace every blunder and let friendship grow.
For in every heartbeat of regret or delight,
Lies a tale waiting, just out of sight!

Echoes in the Silence

In a house where shadows play,
The echo of a sneeze holds sway.
A lizard laughs, a mouse sings low,
While the walls just shake their heads, you know.

The curtains sway, they gossip a bit,
About the dog that might just fit.
A cat in silence, eyes like stars,
Dreams of sneaking out to bars.

The fridge hums jokes, the floorboards creak,
As if they know the secrets we seek.
Tick-tock, the clock gives a wink,
Mismatched socks in the drawer, don't blink!

Each room a stage with drama and flair,
Rhythms of life dance through the air.
So here's to whispers, and giggles they lend,
In the corners where laughter will never end.

Whispers of the Forgotten

In forgotten corners, the dust bunnies roam,
They share wild tales of their ancient home.
With twinkling eyes and a curious wink,
They plot great schemes over a glass of pink.

The cobwebs weave stories of old,
Of socks that escaped, and bold tales retold.
A carpet sings with a moth's delight,
As hidden treasures emerge in the night.

The windows laugh when the wind starts to howl,
Imitating cats, a ghostly growl.
Old books chuckle, placed neatly on shelves,
Their spines so proud, telling tales of themselves.

The laughter persists in the cracks of the floor,
As echoes of problems dissolve into lore.
So join the fun, in this space so alive,
Where whimsy and wonder always thrive.

Shadows in the Bricks

In a house made of bricks, a game is afoot,
Where shadows play tag, oh what a hoot!
They twist and they turn, with sneaky delight,
And run for cover when it turns into night.

The cracks on the wall hold a secret or two,
Of a runaway shoe and a lost rubber shoe.
A shadow gives chase, trying to find,
The left one it lost, too soundly a bind.

Glances exchanged between beams of the roof,
As a mouse tells a story, the ultimate proof.
There's mischief afoot, under each dusty chair,
Where shadows and socks dance without a care.

So let's raise a glass to the mischief they make,
The laughter that tumbles, the joy they awake.
In corners and edges, like magic they thrive,
Shadows in bricks, forever alive!

Secrets of the Closed Doors

Behind those closed doors, a mystery hums,
With whispers and giggles and sneaky thumbs.
A sock puppet plays a leading role,
Where secrets exchange, in a laugh they troll.

The light switch clicks, oh what a surprise!
A dance party starts, with twinkling eyes.
A broom joins in, takes the lead for a spin,
While the doorframes shake, letting fun seep in.

What's cooking up there? A stew of old shoes?
Or a banquet of laughter, with giggles to choose?
A bathtub sings softly, serenades the day,
While the sink regales with tales in its spray.

So here's to those doors, those keepers of cheer,
Where laughter is whispered, resonating near.
The secrets they hold, keep our hearts warm,
In the sanctuary of fun, they always transform.

Remembering Through the Void

In the attic lies a sock,
A relic from a fashion shock.
Invisible echoes from the past,
Wondering how long it will last.

A ghostly snicker from the chair,
Did it just move or is that air?
Forgotten snacks under the rug,
Oh, the mice must be so snug!

Lunchboxes filled with mismatched tin,
Hiding memories of what has been.
Eyes stare back from dusty frames,
Whispering secrets, calling names.

Laughter spills in shades of gray,
From jigsaw puzzles gone astray.
Beneath the paint, a mystery lies,
Chasing laughter, where silence lies.

Hidden Harmonies Within

A melody plays on a squeaky door,
Its laugh echoes on the wooden floor.
Two socks dance in an unseen waltz,
Making shadows that shift and pulse.

Underneath the stairs, you hear a song,
A chorus of dust that's waited long.
The fridge hums in a comical tune,
Imagining meals that left too soon.

Chairs gossip while we're all away,
About the socks that went astray.
A headless broom makes a playful sweep,
In the old house that chuckles in sleep.

Ticking clocks with a quirky beat,
Winking at dreams beneath their feet.
Laughter echoes where spirits play,
In the corners, where shadows sway.

Sighs of the Enclosed

A closet sighs with each pulled shoe,
Whispering tales of a style askew.
In the bathroom, the sink's a crooner,
Polishing mirrors like a good tuner.

The wallpaper hums an old refrain,
Of parties once held, now just a stain.
Worn-out towels in a stacked display,
Dream of sunbathing on a holiday.

Here's the fridge, with an ice cream plea,
Begging for friends, 'come and see me!'
While cereal boxes gossip so loud,
About the days when they felt proud.

From behind the walls, laughter swells,
In all the stories that time retells.
Forgotten treasures and lost delight,
Sighs of memories dance through the night.

Messages from the Abyss

In the depths of the drawer, a sock cries out,
Its mate on a mission, wandering about.
Each crumpled note, a silly plight,
A treasure map to snack time delight.

The toaster pops with a charm divine,
Whispering secrets about bread, oh so fine.
Eggs in the fridge giggle and tease,
Tickled by worries of a royal freeze.

Old books chuckle in dusty rows,
Where parchment dreams of long-lost prose.
Outrageous tales of jelly spills,
Hidden under the warmth of sill.

From shadows cast by the kitchen lamp,
Lurking spoons with a mischievous stamp.
Messages float in the evening air,
Where laughter holds the tales we share.

Parables from the Shadows

In corners dark where whispers play,
The jokes of ghosts invite the day.
They chuckle soft, then break the hush,
With puns that make the bravest blush.

An echo of a laughter near,
It tickles thoughts, brings forth a cheer.
A tale of cats in hats so fine,
Stolen snacks? Just half a line.

Behind the drywall, secrets stew,
Like coffee grounds left in a brew.
The clatter of laughter, pure delight,
As shadows dance with glee at night.

A clock ticks slow, but time's a jest,
With humor playing all the best.
Invisible hands raise up a glass,
To toast the fun that shadows cast.

Heartstrings Across the Divide

Strumming chords on unseen strings,
Each note a quirk, the laughter sings.
An aria of blunders bright,
It floats on air and takes to flight.

What's that? A skit through the cracks?
A chorus of mischief, loud attacks?
With every punchline deftly thrown,
The walls respond with giggles grown.

A serenade from rooms afar,
With playful jibes, it raises the bar.
They trade wisecracks like old pals,
While shadows sway, they laugh and pals.

Behind thick plaster and paint so bold,
The tales of folly dare to unfold.
Each quip resounds, then disappears,
Yet lingers sweetly through the years.

The Resonance of Hidden Truths

A riddle penned in ghostly ink,
Makes spirits giggle, makes mortals think.
In every creak, a punchline hides,
And echoes bounce from sides to sides.

What's this? A prank just out of reach,
The quirkiest lessons that they teach.
Whispers fly like confetti bright,
Filling the air with sheer delight.

From shadows cast in midnight's glow,
The humor flows and starts to grow.
A game of wit beneath the tiles,
With laughter echoing for miles.

So turn the knob, and peek inside,
Where secrets and giggles oft collide.
For humor rings from darkened nooks,
And fills the heart, just like good books.

Serenades Underneath the Facade

With a tap and a clap beneath the floor,
The serenade begins once more.
A tangle of tunes from ups and downs,
Silly rhymes and puzzling frowns.

A soft refrain of socks that roam,
And rubber ducks that call this home.
In hidden corners, giggles twist,
Where every muffled laugh insists.

The jester's hat, it drapes so low,
While shadows dance with coy bravado.
A melody of humor sweet,
Bubbling forth from empty seats.

So listen close to what you hear,
A symphony of joy and cheer.
Amid the silence, fun will spark,
As shadows play their endless arc.

Beneath the Cloak of Stillness

In silence they chatter, what a surprise,
Whispers of mischief, oh, what fun lies!
The pots and pans giggle, the chairs start to sway,
While dust bunnies plot an escape for the day.

Ticking clocks conspire, they strike a grand pose,
Winking at shadows, in secret they doze.
A creaky floorboard tips, then jumps with delight,
In this quiet circus, the night's full of light.

Curtains are gossiping, colors so bold,
Telling old secrets, their stories untold.
Beneath the calm surface, a ruckus ensues,
In the realm of stillness, funny tales amuse.

So listen intently, don't miss out the show,
Behind every silence, there's laughter to grow.
The world may seem empty, but oh, what a blast,
In the stillness of night, the fun is amassed.

Sentiments in the Stillness

In the hush of the room, a sock starts to dance,
An enthusiastic lefty, forgetting its chance.
The curtains giggle, they're all in a spin,
While the dust motes bust moves, it's a real win-win.

Pots chuckle softly, sharing their fate,
Who knew a ladle could carry such weight?
Furry little critters with voices so sweet,
Taunt the sleepy broom that can't move its feet.

The clock grins and chimes, "I'm still ticking fine!"
Amidst all the laughter, it pours out the wine.
Each tick is a riddle, each tock is a jest,
Life's comical moments are simply the best.

So here in this quiet, we find the delight,
In whispers and chuckles, oh, what a sight!
Sentiments simmer, in light and in shade,
In stillness, the laughter and joy are displayed.

Unseen Echoes of Belief

While shadows take conversations in the dimming light,
A carrot starts bragging, "I'm the healthiest bite!"
Mops and brooms chuckle, cleaning with flair,
As the fridge hums tunes, raising spirits in the air.

Floors creak with laughter, a melody so sweet,
Every little whisper becomes a cool beat.
The wobbly table keeps offering advice,
"Don't let the pie cool; it's too nice to slice!"

Rugs throw a party, fiber party hats,
While the windows are gossiping, what of the cats?
In this unseen realm where laughter's are rife,
Even in stillness, there's a party for life.

So let the walls echo with giggles and cheer,
In this world of silence, the fun's always near.
You never can tell how a quiet night drinks,
With unseen echoes that play with our links.

An Ode to the Afflicted

In corners they nestle, a laugh and a sigh,
The furniture's frowning, oh, why must we try?
A pudding's lament, "Why must I be sweet?"
As the bowls tap their edges, they dance to the beat.

Chairs sit in silence, knitting tales of despair,
While the couches complain of their permanent wear.
The dust settles slowly, in patterns so grand,
Each speck holds a story; you just need to understand.

"Oh dear, it's quite tragic, the plight of the broom,"
It wishes for glamour, not just to sweep gloom.
Yet laughter erupts from the cracks in the walls,
As the felines plan pranks, and the curtain just falls.

So here's to the downtrodden, the weary and worn,
In silence, let joy be happily born.
For even the afflicted can find a fine jest,
A wink and a chuckle, in stillness we're blessed.

Murmurs of the Bound

In the shadows they gather, quite a show,
Whispers of mischief, secretive flow.
Laughter erupts from behind painted bricks,
Echoes of pranks and clever little tricks.

Chuckles escape from a creaky old door,
What happens in silence? Oh, there's so much more!
A tap on the wall, a nudge from the floor,
They're planning a party, who could ask for more?

Jokes travel swiftly like a breeze in the night,
Conspiracies spin from the left and the right.
Guess who stole cookies? Oh, what a delight!
The plot thickens proudly, such a comical sight!

So let them be heard, as they cackle and cheer,
Life's fun in the corners where laughter is near.
Murmurs of the bound, they craft tales so bright,
Behind those old walls, the jesters ignite.

Chronicles of the Overlooked

Stuck in the attic, a mouse in a hat,
He spins wild tales of his friendship with cat.
Forgotten old socks join in with their musings,
While dust bunnies dance, those crafty accusers.

An old dusty box, filled with letters and dreams,
Whispers of stories, or so it seems.
Socks covering secrets, they giggle and plot,
What once was neglected, now turns to a lot.

They trade bits of gossip at the break of the day,
Chattering happily, come join in the play!
Once prisoners of fabric, they now run the game,
Chronicles flourish, none of them feel shame!

Oh, the pranks that they've hatched, oh, the tales left untold,
The rants of the overlooked grow bolder, more bold.
And laughter erupts, with no hints of despair,
In this world of forgotten, we find joy everywhere.

Resonances of the Overcome

From the cracks in the plaster, a chuckle breaks free,
In a house under pressure, it's more fun, you see.
With every creak of the floorboards, they conspire,
The voices unite in a comedic choir.

A potato chip crumbles with every good laugh,
And old tattered curtains become the new staff.
Together they chat, like true comrades in crime,
Echoes of humor tickle the heart every time.

The light flickers softly, a wink from the light,
Shadows all giggle, as they sway through the night.
No sorrow, just stories of things passed along,
Resonances crafting a very sweet song.

So listen attentively, as they weave and they twist,
For laughter is painted on the background of mist.
In rooms cloaked in silence, the glee overcomes,
From the cracks of the walls, their jubilance hums.

The Language of the Lost

What happened to the socks? They banter and play,
In delightful confusion, they spin tales each day.
The dryer can't catch them; they're lost in the spin,
A game of hide and seek, oh, where to begin?

Chattering echoes in a cereal box,
Half-eaten stories from rebellious flocks.
Old batteries chuckle, 'We were heroes once,'
In the kingdom of lost, they've got quite the dunce.

Hushed little whispers, behind cabinets tall,
A language of laughter, where jesters enthrall.
The mugs shake with glee in their cupboardy lair,
As the chips on the dishes just giggle and stare.

So join in this ruckus, this wily charade,
For the lost have the wisdom of fun that won't fade.
In the home of the quirky, each nook shares a jest,
The language of laughter is all for the best.

Timeless Echoes

In the attic, a ghost says hi,
With a broomstick as his alibi.
He's sweeping up dust, making a scene,
Looking for socks that once were clean.

The old clock laughs, it's gone out of time,
It chimes in the key of a nursery rhyme.
Lost in the echoes of old, sweet tunes,
Dancing with shadows, beneath the moons.

A cat sneaks by, wearing a hat,
Pretending to be a sophisticated brat.
While the curtains giggle, flapping with glee,
Embracing the silliness, wild and free.

Old chairs creak like they've got tales,
Of tea parties with invisible snails.
They gossip all day, rustling their arms,
Oh, the fun of these quirky charms!

Reverberations of the Past

A cupboard speaks, but don't be scared,
It tells of snacks that a bear once shared.
Echoes of laughter, a raucous cheer,
As spoons in the drawer jive without fear.

The wallpaper whispers sweet, silly rhymes,
Cracking up when it hears the crimes.
Of cookies devoured by sneaky hands,
Making delicious, crumbly plans.

The sofa sighs, a tired old chap,
It dreams of the naps where it took a nap.
With each creak and groan, it tells its tale,
Of countless turmoils and grand cookies' sale.

And in each corner, a shadow plays,
Fingering the dust, a game of charades.
They trick the cat; she falls for their spell,
The antics of old, oh, they work so well!

Fables in the Darkness

In the closet, a dragon snores loud,
Storing secrets under the shrouded cloud.
It dreams of kittens in crowns of lace,
Who laugh at the gloom with a purring grace.

A sock puppet claims to be a sage,
Sharing wisdom from a plastic age.
While in the shadows, the dust bunnies scheme,
Plotting wild tales, lost in a dream.

The nightlight blinks, a silent friend,
Guiding mischief, till the night ends.
It glows in the chaos of toys on display,
While giggles burst forth, leading the way.

A tricycle giggles, two wheels in a spin,
Telling the tales of where it's been.
Each playful spin reveals a new dance,
In the circus of life, what a chance!

The Call of the Concealed

Underneath the stairs, a party's afoot,
With mismatched socks, and a mouse in a suit.
They toast to the cheese, oh what a delight,
Squeaks and squeals fill the starry night.

The shadows all gather, a rowdy bunch,
Trading old stories over a lunch.
Kitchen towels wave, serving up laughs,
As forgotten old mugs hold their own staffs.

The air is thick with a hint of jam,
While lanterns flicker, banishing glam.
A dust motes' dance, a glittering fleet,
In the hands of the time, everything's sweet.

And when morning breaks with a sleepy yawn,
The secret lives fade, but the fun lingers on.
For what's life without a twist of the strange?
Each nook and cranny holds tales that exchange!

Secrets in the Silence

In corners dark, where giggles hide,
A secret mishap, no one can abide.
A cat in a hat, a mouse in a shoe,
Lurking in silence, oh what can they do?

The neighbor's parrot tells tales so grand,
Of haunted cupcakes from a far-off land.
A whisper or two, a chuckle or three,
What happens at night? Just you wait and see!

A cactus wearing socks sways to the beat,
In shadows it dances, oh, isn't that sweet?
A sock drawer's waltz, with unmatched pairs,
They gossip so loudly; who really cares?

A giggle escapes from behind the door,
A secret dance party, oh, the fun's in store!
With jellybeans flying and confetti in hand,
A world of pure laughter, so whimsically planned.

The Sound of Distant Dreams

In dreamland balloons float high and bright,
Pigs wear top hats, all curious in flight.
An elephant trumpets a jazzy old tune,
While cupcakes pirouette under the moon.

With whispers of waffles and chocolate delight,
They chatter of breakfast till morning's first light.
A squirrel with glasses recites poetry,
To macaroni ducks who listen with glee.

The tickle of giggles in soft, silky air,
Has a llama in pajamas doing a flair.
Between clouds of marshmallows, they swing and sway,
Those dreams sounding softly, all blissful and gay.

While shadows hold secrets in their cozy embrace,
The sound of delight puts a smile on my face.
In distant realms, where the funny things gleam,
The night is alive with the sound of a dream.

Stories Woven in Silence

Behind the curtain, a story unfolds,
A grumpy old ghost, or so it is told.
With a big bag of tricks and a rickety chair,
He searches for laughter, but finds only air.

A tape measure runs, seeking all it can reach,
To measure tall tales that no one will preach.
A hiccuping shadow, a giggling breeze,
Weaving a fabric of stories with tease.

The cupboard is chattering; it wants to chat,
About the wild cat that chased a worn mat.
With secrets like jelly, all squishy and bright,
These stories weave laughter throughout the night.

As whispers curl up like a cat on a log,
The stories take form of a funny old fog.
Each twist and each turn, a burst of delight,
In silence, they bubble; oh what a sight!

Soft Hums Beneath the Surface

In bubble wrap trenches, the whispers reside,
A battle of giggles is fought with great pride.
Under the carpet, a symphony hums,
While socks plot a caper; oh, here it comes!

A smirk from the fridge, as leftovers joke,
While a can of beans plays the role of a bloke.
With pots and pans dancing a melodic spree,
The kitchen's a concert, come listen and see!

The couch makes a snicker, the pillows join in,
A soft little chorus, where laughter can spin.
Each creak in the floorboards a tale to impart,
Of funny adventures, a beat of the heart.

And beneath all the chaos, a joy we can't trace,
The soft hums of laughter put smiles on our face.
So come join the fun, where giggles ignite,
In secretive nooks, the world feels just right.

www.ingramcontent.com/pod-product-compliance
Lightning Source LLC
Chambersburg PA
CBHW070004300426
43661CB00141B/208